Troupers

Keith Hutson

smith|doorstop

Published 2018 by
Smith|Doorstop Books
The Poetry Business
Campo House
54 Campo Lane
Sheffield S1 2EG

ISBN 978-1-910367-83-4

Designed and Typeset by Tim Morris
Printed by Biddles Books

Smith|Doorstop Books are a member of Inpress:
www.inpressbooks.co.uk. Distributed by NBN International,
Airport Business Centre, 10 Thornbury Road, Plymouth, PL6 7PP

The Poetry Business gratefully acknowledges the support
of Arts Council England.

Supported by
ARTS COUNCIL
ENGLAND

Contents

For Robert and Adele

'We were so poor, my dad couldn't afford homing pigeons – he had a budgie on elastic.'

— Les Dawson

Revival

Like the funniest of men, he had that look:
bad health crossed with indestructibility.
Fans would slap and cuddle him.

It takes a certain type of body to appear,
night after night, as if a gang's manhandled
it into a dinner suit; face folded
like a heart attack was homing in.

It was. But he'd soaked several up already;
recovered with a crack:
Treading boards is my best exercise!

After the last, wrapped in an overcoat
on Blackpool prom, he'd seemed robust enough,
just pale. And people like him, whose fathers

died in harness, whose mothers bore silent,
determined lives, they never bow out barely used.
One way or another they sweat buckets,
under stress, and make that state hilarious.

That's why we wet ourselves when they collapse
at the Palladium. And why it's only right
to raise another smile, to bring them back.

Tiddly Om Pom Pom

i.m. Mark Sheridan 1865–1918

Hit after hit, he couldn't kill his gift
for gaiety, the flip, untroubled stuff
men whistled on their way to war – tunes tough
enough for trenches, tears. They made him rich
and wretched, those shape-shifters in his head,
imagined like Beethoven's 5th, dashed out
another *Stop Yer Ticklin', Jock!* instead,
and more top sales to get morose about.

Some say the mediocre can't be spoiled
by anti-climax, but our songsmith died
a death to still all choruses: appalled
beyond condolence by *Beside The Seaside*,
he declared *This last confection breaks my heart*,
and blew his brains out in a Glasgow park.

Straight Man

You think you could be me, don't you?
The nobody who's only there to prop
the patter up. The one who, deadpan,
asks the obvious to set the silly answers free.

You think you could be me but better.
Make more of an effort. Be a super-feed.
Do so much more than look disdainful.

Try it, then. Try not to smile.
Be subliminal lit by a bank of lights.
Try keeping control, reining in an idiot;
forcing the pace so he can fly.

Try to pitch a put-down perfectly
and, backstage, be the chipper one who copes
with nerves, neurosis. Do the admin too.

Try this for size: the difference between us,
you and me, is I *pretend* I'm dull.
And that barrel of laughs who acts
like he should be locked up –
he is. Try being the key.

The Man With The Xylophone Skull

i.m. Professor Cheer 1879–1938

Let's hear it for this prematurely bald
headmaster: struck by the disquieting fact
his crown – hit with a brass door handle – could
resound, a bell, his temples too, he taught

himself to scale an octave, frontal bone
to back, and at the Christmas show knocked out
a carol, *Ding Dong Merrily*, performed,
he quipped (as teachers do) *on high!* But what

should have stayed a daft percussion act at school –
festive morale – didn't. He went on tour,
six years – concussion, mild first, getting worse, till
memory went with his pension, somewhere

old wolves paw at stone, ravens croak, snow falls
on carcasses through which a cold wind howls.

Hylda

i.m. Hylda Baker 1909–1986

Nine was the age the likes of her learnt
how to lip-read at the mill;
to flap their silent mouths in turn.

But Hylda found her voice inside this act,
talent that kept her in pink gins for years:
a *popular comedienne*, bottom of the bill.

Funny, then, to be described by Delfont
as an overnight success, *proprietress*
of Pledge's Pickle Factory on ITV.

They said that show went to her head.
Deaf to them, she changed her tipple to a lot
of crème de menthe, bought a bungalow

in Cleveleys, quilted bedroom floor to ceiling,
cocktail bar an opera box, doorbell
singing *Come Back To Sorrento*

as she warned reporters,
Don't be dazzled by the décor –
it's contemporary.

Barred from playing panto dame,
she made her men wear dresses, let them stay
on the condition they were dumb.

Her harem swelled, and neighbours,
outraged yet refined, presented a petition:
Please leave. Thank you.

This prompted the flagpole with
You haven't had the pleasure of me yet
flown every day and twice for matinees.

Spandex at seventy, that bump-and grind
with Arthur Mullard on Top of the Pops,
and then she died, demented,

utterly alone – unmourned
by impresarios and sisterhoods alike.
Nine was the number at her funeral.

Hostess Trolley

Often employed in Alan Ayckbourn plays,
this one, as soon as it was wheeled on stage,
loaded with nibbles, drinkie-poos, began
to concertina. Which it would, when some
fool hadn't locked the catch. Geoffrey, who no
amount of pancake could remould into
a suave young architect, couldn't let go
of it throughout the second act. Where he
went, it went, and the bending made his tight
suit trousers look half-mast. Then his back seized.
During the interval, we tried some holds
and tugs that made it worse. He's still not right,
we've heard: no one from our lot ever sees
him, now he's cast so well for playing bowls.

Glasgow Empire

Yes, it was here the gang show audience
slow-handclapped that girl guide
with laryngitis;

the Beverley Sisters flitted on
then promptly darted off again
to cries of *Christ, there's three of 'em!*

Where else would Eartha Kitt
be forced back out, Ken Dodd
having cut his act in half?

After Des O'Connor fainted
from derision, dragged to safety,
seventy ice creams were counted on his suit.

Even when empty, anger
occupied this auditorium. It bloomed,
silent and black: a storm building to break

above row upon row of folded seats,
all rigid as a nervous herd
before it bolts.

Beyond Belief
i.m. Sid Field 1904–1950

He talked a good trapeze act – in his tights,
hands white with chalk – the best we never saw:
I might even change my mind, mid-air!
Sid had us gazing at those dizzy heights,
and he was there, all swing and sweep, above us,
never mind he hadn't even climbed
the pole, set foot inside a circus
or off terra-firma, ever. Were we blind

to this pretence? Naïve to let such
elevated promises toss reason
to the wind? Or could Sid's flights of fancy catch
and turn the truth? Can words, well-placed, become
so strong they're flesh and sinew on the wing:
not less than, but beyond the real thing?

Civic Theatre

Essential to the town's supply of ham
and never known to not deliver, here
Macbeth, La Cage aux Folles, See How They Run

have all been butchered, served up overdone
to friends and relatives, the latest mayor
essential to the town's supply of ham.

How seamlessly the shows flow into one
homogenous creation – *Who Goes Bare,*
Macbeth, La Cage aux Folles, See How They Run,

but each with unexpected extras in:
startled stagehands, Banquo falling through his chair,
essential to the town's supply of ham.

And every set unfailingly Am Dram –
potted plants, French windows, even in *Hair,*
Macbeth, La Cage aux Folles, See How They Run.

Soon it's *The Crucible.* That should be fun.
I'm in the chorus, do support us, we're
essential to the town's supply of ham!
Macbeth! La Cage aux Folles! See How They Run!

Light Brigade

i.m. Macauley's Leaping Infants 1856–1866

Alive, but both legs left at Balaclava,
Lance Corporal Macauley swore he'd rather
starve than beg: perhaps pride came before

and following a fall, for men who'd been
with the Six Hundred and survived. His plan
was martial: muster local urchins lame

from twisted, short or withered limb, club foot,
rickets – plus those born whole who later got
what they deserved – then teach them theirs was not

to reason why, when he said *Jump*, but ask
How high? The Times claimed it could never last,
yet England's Most Unlikely Acrobats

toured ten years without praise: laughter, instead,
kept both Macauley and his army fed.

Vera

Even then it was a name for adults,
not an eight year old. In the backward stream,
worse at maths than me, she had no father

and a limp. Her mum was Mrs Worthington,
so we'd stand at her broken gate and sing
Don't put your daughter on the stage, then run

until, one teatime, more worse for wear
than normal, Mrs W came round to shout
our antics at my dad. He listened –

placidly for him – before responding
Fair enough, but she's hardly Tiny Tim.
I had a stab at fending off the strap with:

Vera doesn't mind, she says she likes it.
Her mum's drunk all the time and starves the dog.
If you don't hit me I'll apologize.

Before they took her into care, Vera performed
a vent act for the teacher with her Sindy doll
to Neil Sedaka's *Where The Music Takes Me,*

ending on a *happy happy happy happy day!*
that left the class light-headed with respect
and must have taken years of practise.

My Old Man

i.m. Ephraim Barraclough 1853–1906

Tell him three traits, and he'd impersonate
your dad. This chip off everyone's old block
possessed, let's say, a patriarchal knack
to take a parent's essence, flesh it out
– the full Monty, Tom, Albert, Harry, Dick –
rough or benign, for better or for worse:
offspring whose hurt returned took flight in tears;
beloveds got a flash of hero back.

He didn't do his own though: *Little point*
aping a fellow if the audience don't
know him. Neither did Ephraim: *He left.*
That's that. Most of us let it go, except
a postman who arrived at the stage door,
ashes and cap in hand: *Your father, sir.*

The Call Of The Wild

i.m. Percy Edwards 1908–1996

Has anybody risen from such bleakness –
a chicken in the chapel pageant,
cancelled? Then Old Mother Hubbard's
hopeful dog, Ipswich infants' panto:
Make an effort, little Edwards, said the head.

Who could predict, once broken in,
our boy would grow to be the perfect
Suffolk Punch, Black Mountain, Saddleback,
or any livestock loud and proud required?
But Percy wasn't just a walking farm,

he stopped Sir David Attenborough in his tracks:
A kookaburra? Ten miles from West Ham?
Guess who gave vent to pheasants, cock
and hen, for Carry On ... whichever one it was;
pitched *Orca* to perfection; Peter O'Toole's parrot

and a stag at bay in *Ivanhoe*, lamenting
wasted blood. He hissed in *Alien* at Ripley,
while those old enough still talk of how they hid
behind the sofa from his lion's roar
for Campbell's tinned meatballs, but join

their children, carried off by songbirds Kate Bush
dropped into her enigmatic airs. All him.
More basic was a goat bleat, *On The Buses*,
no match for his wolf which, at the Windmill's
non-stop nude revue, gave everyone the willies.

I recall his coos, plump as a dove's,
on *David Nixon's Magic Box;* and mum's LP,
played as she helped me shepherd plastic sheep
across the rug – my dad, a stockman's son, unhappy
we'd become so distant from the land.

Accept No Imitations
i.m. J D Plummer 1846–1901

Do your colleagues call you a control freak?
Fuck 'em. Abandoned on the first night
by his cast, J D played every character
himself: Dick Turpin, victims, innkeeper
and black-eyed daughter Bess, Dick's worn-out horse,
also called Bess, and black (this did cause
confusion), Tom the Ostler who betrayed them,
weeping Widow Shelley, Tyburn hangman,

and it ran for fifteen months, through Glossop,
Leeds and York, till he collapsed banging two
coconuts together at a gallop,
then went bankrupt, then insane. Worth it, though,
to show incompetents what can be done
by one who stands, delivers, falls, alone.

Widow Twankey

Daybreak kills the lights along the pier.
Mist at the deep end lifts
and there the Playhouse hangs – that wreck
where last night was the deadest yet: a dozen
plus a seagull on the follow-spot
that took a dislike to his wig,
drawing blood for a finale.

A rock supports a bottle drained of single malt,
and there's a sea breeze dropping salt into his scab.
He's disgraced himself, a cock-stride
from the toilets on the prom –
would have tried to find a gag in that,
the laughter there, back when
he had a name enough to care.

Sea weeps into the dame-shaped crater
made when he lost consciousness,
sometime after they'd paid him off
and said they'll not be wanting him next winter
'cos you're shit, love. Had he thought it might be time
to hang his frock up? B&Q take people on
who haven't got a pension.

Shingle trickles down his knickers.
A crushed shell rubs between the scaffolds
of his bra. Around him everything takes shape
as dawn becomes another morning, and it dawns
on him he didn't rip his cheque up on a whim.
Sleek as a private limousine, the tide arrives.
He bows a bit, and starts to wade.

The Man Who Killed Houdini

i.m. J. Gordon Whitehead 1895–1954

I was thirty. Still a student. Immature.
The only chains I'd wrestled with were
theoretical. And what a lark to lie
my way into his dressing room. To see
him semi-naked, dabbing pancake
on his face. Average, unshackled – no great
shakes. Like me. But foolish – happy to be
hit: *Hard as you can, boy.* Boy? *Just give me
time to brace myself.* Like hell! Four
punches to the stomach, he was on the floor,
doubled-up and writhing. Not an act.
Ruptured appendix – boy – get out of that!
His tomb's impressive, but my pauper's grave
attracts the masses. People are depraved.

A Funny Thing Happened...

i.m. Frankie Howerd 1917–1992

Every quip fresh from the quipperies!
Fresh? Alright, let's just say *pre-loved*.
But you try being new, looking like me –
the man who lied about his age, adding years
to match the lines. Try sweating for six decades –
comeback after comeback since your first
No! Missus! Nay! Thrice nay! Titter ye not!

Before the flops, I thought who wouldn't flock
to watch a gossip in a toupé waffle?
What's not to like? *Face like a bankrupt nag,*
a critic said. My mother, actually.
Bless her, we shared so much. But even she
had no idea her son was gay: in those days
it was bitter out. I hid it well. No?

I must confess backstage perhaps I fell
a little short of coy. Clinically depressed,
it seemed to help. What didn't was a shrink
from Harley Street who fed me LSD
before a romp around his attic every weekend.
Best cure for your stage fright,
he'd cackle, catching his breath.

Triumphs? *Frankie Howerd Meets The Bee Gees*
wasn't one. Thank God for the Oxbridge set
who dug me up again. *Alternative*, they called me –
how we laughed. A judge dug up my lover too.
Exhumed him from our mock Egyptian tomb.
Now there's a tale that might have packed 'em in.
Too late – my lips are sealed.

Saddled

i.m. Harris 'Wonder Horse' Fitzpatrick 1803–1847

Born to play the front end, under hessian
and felt, Harris expressed such human-equine
feelings, every toss, nod, shake, incline

said more than Hamlet at his most verbose
because, once Harris was immersed in horse,
the stammer didn't matter, for his voice

was body-language – nuzzle, jerk and butt –
a dumb-show of stubborn, affectionate,
skittish, morose. But when he'd got the bit

between his teeth, what started as a hobby
took the reins till, out of season, he
would shy away from words, and nobody

could coax him back: always a danger when
someone feels ill at ease in their own skin.

The World's Greatest Whistler

i.m. Ronnie Ronalde 1923–2015

Listen, this man sent shivers down
Sinatra's spine. Marilyn Monroe
spoke of a state of grace.
But let's go back

to when a boy in Islington blew
Tales From The Vienna Woods
for food, and borrowed birdsong
to return it spotless.

Then the teenager who made
a shilling every *triple trill*,
enough to fly Stateside where stadia
turned into temples to *The Suited Flute*.

Rock 'n' Roll drowned Ronnie out,
but whistles as pristine as his
don't disappear. They slip
between the living and the lost;

pipe up again so someone may think
tinnitus at first,
then shut their eyes, untroubled,
in a meadow never mown.

Crowd Control

i.m. The Bryn Pugh Sponge Dancers c.1855

A soft act to follow? Nothing did –
they always went on last, the *buffer* spot,
when people put their coats on, filtered out
with half an eye on them: *Our job*, Bryn said,
*was to prevent a crush, a bottleneck
of bodies heading home. We weren't much good,
see? Some saw that straight away and caught
the early tram.* Still, I suppose a few would

hang on till the end, hoping for more than
mattresses three women sank into, sprang from.
There *is* more, though: Bryn married all of them,
you could say on a triple-rebound, then
wrote a memoir, *Ups And Downs*, confessing two
had been his daughters, and the other knew.

Street Cred

i.m. Tony Warren 1936–2016

Pendlebury bred its women wartime
tough. Mams, aunties, grans, *the flamin' neighbours* –
warriors with nowt, who'd never ration
what they were: gossip, stoic, glamour puss;

grafter, scrubber, put-upon. They brought you
up, my lad – Eccles Grammar clever,
lippy, witty, out-and-proud before
it was allowed: love on the never-never.

Future? Fallow at first. *Children's Hour*, a script
for Biggles and, expelled from acting class,
a spot of choreography in strip
clubs – hardly Moulin Rouge, but ready cash.

Later, sleeping on a slow train home from
Thanks, but no in London, you awoke – and how!
I'll write about Florizel Street! Hang on,
a tea lady (relation, maybe?) saw

the flaw: *Sounds like a disinfectant, son.*
So, Coronation. Chicken? Could you get that
back in '59? Not down your way, young man,
barely turned twenty-one, about to take

those matriarchs and make them Elsie, Ena,
Annie ... Ken? Wrong gender, kid, but maybe
he was you: bright boy; back-alley dreamer.
Light of Manchester. Making history.

Here's Looking At You

i.m. Alice Wolfenden 1861–1913

Chaplin called movement *liberated thought.*
No words required. *Action is all.* But what
if you distil a lifetime's liveliness –
the ducks and dives, embraces, feints; compress
every advance, retreat, escape, into
one concentrated stare, directed through
the theatre's gloom; let your eyes only tell
a tale of non-stop doings – heaven, hell?

Alice mastered this. Completely still, she'd throw
her gaze across the footlights. Those who
held it were transported – felt again
all that had lifted, stirred or broken them.
Hers was the first act women came in groups
to watch, and sob. We men studied our boots.

Brass Band

Bottom line? Seconds into *Sailing*
I'm in tears. Two bars, as a rule, before
the waters break and all my sorrows
drown, diffuse into church hall,
assembly room. It works as well for any tune
dipped in your mournful warmth.

I'm trying to say I love you, and I don't care
if you hit me with *The Stripper* or *Hey Jude* –
who else takes air to make compassion
hospitals have targets for? Then there's your faces,
blank and only blowing; outfits so all the same,
braided or plain, they break my heart.

I've seen you seated, standing, on the march;
in junior schools fresh and lamentable;
as engineers all male and overweight; Welsh Asians
adding spice to *Bread of Heaven* – and always
I'm delivered back, a boy of four, found on the prom
in Bridlington, not lost, just listening.

The Natural

Married in haste again, his next mistake
was a coach tour of the Trossachs for their
honeymoon. After perhaps the worst week
possible of toilet stops, no sex, her
utter disbelief, *Smith's Happiways* put on
a talent show to top things off. *I know*,
he thought, *I'll sing to her*, and asked the man
on the accordion if he knew
Octopus's Garden. He didn't, but
could have a bash at *Yesterday*. So one
sang one, while one attempted to keep up,
playing the other. Seconds in, she'd gone.
But having left a hundred howling, he
embraced his incompatibility

Family Business

I

Old Mother Riley, Arthur Lucan
in a bonnet, married a woman
half his age who turned into his daughter
every evening on stage.

But when curtains were closed,
she called on better men than him
to strip away the minor role
she played.

II

Albert Burdon dressed his son up
as his Ugly Sister.
When not preoccupied with balls,
their bond was brittle
as a crystal slipper.

III

Thank God for Jimmy Clitheroe,
four feet three inches of propriety,
who wore his cap and shorts
for over fifty years, but never dragged
his mum into the act.

The day they buried her,
he tucked into sufficient pills
to kill the boy
he could no longer bear to be.

Clever Bugger

i.m. Bob Monkhouse 1928–2003

Why did we laugh, but never love you, Bob?
Some claimed you came across as insincere.
So what? You were a comic, not the pope.
Perhaps that calculated gulp before
each punchline, patter too precision-made,
anecdotes too pleased with one another,
plus your business acumen and tan, said
Clever Bugger never *National Treasure*

till, with weeks to live, bloated and slow from
drugs, you begged all men, on *Parkinson*,
to take a prostate test. Too late for you,
but what a warm performance, funny too –
it won us critics over there and then:
smart move, Bob, dying *such a decent man.*

Lament

i.m. Sing Something Simple 1959–2001

Sunday afternoons gave up the ghost
to this: a lone accordion
held little comfort as the theme tune
faded into half an hour of shadow,
cast across the country
by the Light Programme.

It came to rival *Songs of Praise*
for sudden deaths:
the tender preface could have been
Why not lie back
and ponder ways to end
it all without alarming others.

At eight I joined a boxing club
that met when it was on the radiogram.
An expert might conjecture
I preferred a fat lip to Cliff Adams
and his choir, for over forty years
kept artificially alive:

that's ten prime ministers,
all looking grim. The folk who tuned in
first, from choice, are falling now.
But they were tough – took any measure
of *make-do* thrown at them,
could survive on airwaves if required.

Memory Man

i.m. Herbert Fernandez 1813–1898

We all recalled his glory days, before
grey whiskers: *Ask me anything!* Facts filled
Hull Hippodrome, staccato-sharp and sure –
no doubt about the data he revealed;
his mind as rich as any bank – robust
beyond belief. But why, in later life, when
age ate his reserves and he stood at a loss,
did no one treasure Herbert less, or blame
him playing to our faith instead of trust?
Why weren't his nightly clangers billed, at best,
as laughable: what makes ovation last?
Let's call it love, and hope, when we become
befuddled by our audience, uncertain,
our performance isn't mocked, but smiled upon.

Acknowledgements

Thanks are due to the editors of the following publications, in which some of these poems, or early versions, first appeared or are forthcoming:
The High Window, The Interpreter's House, London Grip, The Manhattan Review, The North, Stand, Poetry Salzburg Review, The Fortnightly Review.

'Tiddly Om Pom Pom' won 2nd place in Carol Ann Duffy's Sonnet Competition, Manchester Metropolitan University 2016
'Civic Theatre' won 3rd place in the Poetry Business Yorkshire Prize 2015
'Vera' was Commended in the Mclellan Prize 2016
'The Call Of The Wild' was Commended in the Cornwall Poetry Competition 2016
'The Natural' was Commended in the Poetry Space Competition 2017

Heartfelt thanks to Ann and Peter Sansom for all their support and encouragement, and to Michael Symmons Roberts for his guidance and inspiration.

Special thanks to Carol Ann Duffy for her generosity, and for her belief in me.